Tudors

1453	Ottoman Turks capture Constantinople; European countries look for other routes to buy spices
1485	Battle of Bosworth – Henry Tudor is crowned Henry VII
1487-88	Diaz sails from Lisbon right round South Africa
1492	Columbus discovers the West Indies
1497	Cabot discovers Newfoundland, Canada
1497-98	Vasco da Gama sails from Portugal to India
1500	The Portuguese discover Brazil
1506	The Spanish start to have sugar plantations in America
1513	Battle of Flodden against the Scots
1516	African slave traffic to the sugar plantations begins
1517	Martin Luther begins the Reformation
1519-21	Cortes conquers Mexico
1519	Magellan leads the first expedition to go round the world
1525	Tyndale translates the Bible into English
1528	The Spanish conquer Peru
1534	Act of Supremacy - Henry VIII makes himself head of the Church of England
1536	Wales united to England
1536-39	Monasteries are sold off
1545	Council of Trent: Catholic Church begins to reform itself
1558	Calais taken back by the French
1567	Mary Queen of Scots gives throne of Scotland to James
1577	Drake becomes the second person to go round the world
1584	Raleigh starts English colonies in Virginia
1588	The Armada fleet of Philip II of Spain attempts to invade England but is defeated
1602-03	The East India Company founded
1603	Scotland united to England, with one king, James I of England (James VI of Scotland)

Tudors

Felicity Hebditch

Evans Brothers Limited

First published in this edition in 2003 by
Evans Brothers Limited
2A Portman Mansions
Chiltern St
London W1U 6NR

Reprinted 2005

Printed in China

A catalogue record for this book is available from
the British Library.

ISBN 0 237 52572 0

Acknowledgements
Design: Ann Samuel
Editorial: Liz Harman
Illustrations: Nick Hawken and Mike White
Production: Jenny Mulvanny

© Evans Brothers Limited 1995

Acknowledgements

For permission to reproduce copyright material,
the author and publishers gratefully acknowledge
the following:

Cover (main & middle)The Ancient Art &
Architecture Collection, (background & top) the
art archive, (bottom) The Weald & Downland
Open Air Museum, Singleton. Title page Hatfield
House/Fotomas Index. page 6 Michael Holford.
page 7 R.Sheridan/The Ancient Art & Architecture
Collection. page 8 Hever Castle Ltd. page 10
R.Sheridan/The Ancient Art & Architecture
Collection. page 11 Hatfield House/Fotomas
Index. page 12 the art archive/National Maritime
Museum. page 13 (top) Michael Holford, (bottom
left and right) The Mary Rose Trust. page 14 the
art archive/New York Public Library. page 15 (top
and bottom left) R.Sheridan/The Ancient Art &
Architecture Collection, (bottom right) Michael
Holford. page 16 the art archive/National
Maritime Museum. page 17 R.Sheridan/The
Ancient Art & Architecture Collection. page 18
Michael Holford, (bottom) The Weald and
Downland Open Air Museum, Singleton. page 19
R.Sheridan/The Ancient Art & Architecture
Collection page 20 the art archive. page 21
R.Sheridan/The Ancient Art & Architecture
Collection. page 22 (top) R.Sheridan/The Ancient
Art & Architecture Collection, (bottom) The Weald
and Downland Open Air Museum, Singleton. page
23 R.Sheridan/The Ancient Art & Architecture
Collection. page 24 (top) R.Sheridan/The Ancient
Art & Architecture Collection, (bottom) The Mary
Rose Trust. page 25 Kentwell Hall. page 26
R.Sheridan/The Ancient Art & Architecture
Collection. page 27 (top) The Mary Rose Trust,
(bottom) R.Sheridan/The Ancient Art &
Architecture Collection. page 28 (top) the art
archive, (bottom) R.Sheridan/The Ancient Art &
Architecture Collection. page 29 (top) The Mary
Rose Trust, (bottom) Hatfield House, Fotomas
Index.

CONTENTS

Henry VII (1485-1509)
m. Elizabeth of York

Margaret
m. James IV of Scotland

Henry VIII (1509-1547)
m. Catherine of Aragon   m. Anne Boleyn   m. Jane Seymour

Mary
m. Louis XII of France
m. Duke of Suffolk

James V of Scotland

Mary I (1553-1558)
m. Philip II of Spain

Elizabeth I
(1558-1603)

Edward VI
(1547-1553)

Lady Jane Grey
m. Lord Guilford Dudley

Mary Queen of Scots

James VI of Scotland,
I of England (1603-1625)

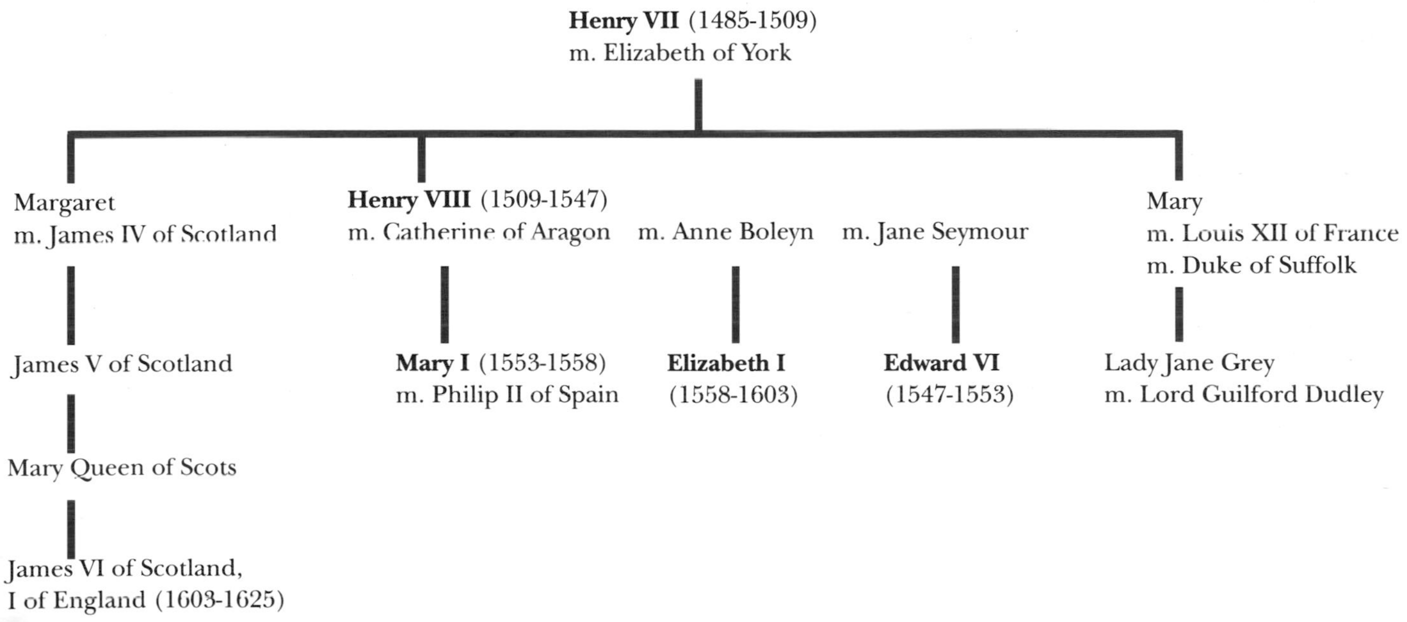

THE FIRST TUDOR KINGS

Who were the Tudors?

The Tudors were the family who ruled England from 1485 to 1603. There were five kings and queens – Henry VII, his son Henry VIII, and his children Edward VI, Mary I and Elizabeth I. They helped to make England and Wales and Scotland in to one country. Life was hard for ordinary people and they died young, from diseases. Some were brave enough to travel to far-away lands in the East and America in the search for gold and spices. New ideas from Europe spread when books began to be printed. Religion, medicine, building, war, everything was changing.

How the Tudors came to the throne

For 30 years before Henry VII became king, there was civil war. Two families, York and Lancaster, fought battles in the 'Wars of the Roses'. The war was called this because the York supporters had a white rose as their symbol and the Lancastrians had a red rose. In 1485 Richard III of York was king. Henry Tudor, a Lancastrian, fought Richard at the battle of Bosworth. Many of Richard's supporters changed sides and he was killed. Richard had been wearing the crown on his helmet and one of Henry's men found it and crowned him Henry VII. Henry married Elizabeth of York and united the two families. He joined the red and white roses to make the new Tudor rose.

The Tudors used the Tower of London to keep their weapons and armour, and prisoners too. Can you see London Bridge in the background?

> *And Richard, who had been king in the morning, was brought back dead, stripped bare and tied up like a hog and all mudspattered.*
>
> from the *Great Chronicle*

Henry VII

A king was always in danger from his enemies. Powerful nobles had castles and private armies, and some plotted against him, saying they had more right to be king. Henry kept his enemies under control by taxing them and making himself richer. He made it illegal for anyone else to have an army and he was the only person who could afford the big new cannon.

The Tudors came from Wales and the Welsh thought of Henry as a Welsh king. Wales was joined to England by the Act of Union of 1536. Scotland and Ireland were separate from England. The Scots made raids on England, stealing whatever they could.

To avoid war, Henry needed to make peace with other countries by signing treaties or agreements. When two countries made a treaty, a marriage was often arranged to seal the agreement. The daughters of kings did not have much choice over whom they married. Their marriages were part of the treaty. Henry VII made his daughter, Mary, marry the king of France, Louis XII, although he was an old man and Mary did not want to marry him. Another daughter, Margaret, had to marry James IV of Scotland. James was killed when he went to war with Margaret's brother, Henry VIII.

Henry VII worked hard to make England peaceful and prosperous. The king did all the work of government. He had a Council to advise him and he chose clever lawyers and churchmen to be his special Privy Council. Parliament only met to make new laws or taxes. Later Tudors made Parliament more important.

Henry VIII

When Henry VII died in 1509, his son Henry VIII became king. Henry VII had saved a great deal of money. Henry VIII was different; he was young and good-looking and he wanted to spend money on enjoying life. He liked expensive clothes, feasts, music and dancing and he was very popular. He did not want to spend his time with the Council, discussing politics. He left the business of running the country to advisers like Cardinal Wolsey and Thomas Cromwell and spent his time hunting, jousting and feasting.

Henry VIII wanted to look grand and spent a great deal of money on clothes. Only rich people were allowed to wear ermine, which is the fur trimming on Henry's coat.

King Henry is handsome. He is very fair. Hearing that King Francis (of France) wore a beard, he allowed his own to grow, and, as it was reddish, he had a beard which looked like gold.

A letter from the Venetian Ambassador (1519)

Henry VII had only gone to war once. In 1492 he captured Etaples from the French and they paid 750,000 crowns to get it back. Henry VIII wanted to bring England power and glory in battle. He went to war with France in 1513, 1522 and 1543 but going to war cost more money than he won. Whenever the English fought the French, the Scots joined in against the English. Henry's army defeated the Scots at the Battle of Flodden but he did not win a lasting peace.

It's true!

Henry VIII owned 55 palaces! He ordered the village of Cuddington in Surrey to be knocked down to make room for a new palace, Nonsuch. He wanted it to be bigger than the King of France's new palace at Fontainebleau.

At this time, Christians in Europe were all Catholics. Many were saying that the Catholic Church needed to make changes. In 1521 a German monk called Martin Luther made a list of reforms. People who supported him were told to obey the Catholic Church but they protested, so they were called Protestants. Arguments began and there were many wars in Europe over religion.

Henry VIII wanted a son to become king after him. England had never had a queen before. Henry had been married to Catherine of Aragon for 20 years but all their children had died except a girl called Mary. Henry fell in love with Anne Boleyn and wanted to divorce Catherine so that he could marry Anne and have a son. But England was a Catholic country and the head of the Church, the Pope, would not allow divorce. So Henry declared that he was the head of the Church in England. He made all Church officials swear that this was true and, if they refused, they were declared to be traitors and executed. Sir Thomas More, one of Henry's ministers, refused to swear and was beheaded.

Anne Boleyn was Henry VIII's second wife. She had been to France and brought back French fashion with her.

Henry's wives

Henry VIII had six wives. His second wife, Anne Boleyn, did not have a son but a girl, Elizabeth. Henry was very disappointed. He said that Anne was a witch and had her beheaded. Next, he married Jane Seymour, who did have a boy, Edward, but she died when he was born. Then Henry married a princess, Anne of Cleeves. Henry had only seen a painting of Anne before they were married. He did not like her so he had the marriage annulled (cancelled out). Henry's fifth wife, Katherine Howard, was young and pretty and Henry soon suspected her of being in love with somebody else so he had her beheaded. Henry was still married to his last wife, Catherine Parr, when he died.

The dissolution of the monasteries

When Henry went to war with France in 1522 he borrowed money and could not afford to repay it. He 'emptied men's pockets' with taxes and the people were angry. The monasteries were rich and owned about a quarter of the land in England and Wales so Henry decided to take over their land and wealth for himself. When he sold it off, it was the biggest sale of land ever.

It's true!

After the dissolution of the monasteries many people were buying land. It was important to have maps showing where people's property was. Christopher Saxton made the first atlas in Britain in 1571.

HENRY VIII'S CHILDREN

Edward VI

Henry VIII died in 1547, leaving England bankrupt. His only son, Edward VI, became king. He was only nine years old and too young to rule so his ministers ruled for him. They were led by the Protector, the Earl of Somerset. Edward had tuberculosis and was ill; everyone knew he would not live for very long.

Because Edward was Henry's only son, the next queen would be Henry's daughter, Mary Tudor. The Earl of Northumberland's son married Lady Jane Grey, one of Henry VII's grandchildren, and King Edward said that Lady Jane should be the queen after him. Edward died when he was just 15 and the Earl of Northumberland had Lady Jane Grey crowned. She was only 16 and did not want to be queen. The people of England supported Mary Tudor. As Mary travelled to London, many people joined her. Northumberland was captured and Queen Jane was taken to the tower and beheaded. She had reigned for just nine days.

Edward VI is said to have smiled only once in his life. He had to obey his advisors and was often ill.

> I *fall on weeping because, whatever else I do but learning, is full of grief, trouble, fear.*
>
> Lady Jane Grey

Mary Tudor married Philip II of Spain and her mother was Spanish. The fashion for wearing dark clothes came from Spain.

Queen Mary

Edward's Council made a law (the Act of Uniformity, 1552) to make everyone Protestant but Mary made it illegal to be a Protestant. She had many Protestants burned at the stake. This shocked many people and made her unpopular. She married King Philip II of Spain and agreed to help Spain in a war against France. Before this war, England owned many parts of France. France won the war and took back Calais, the last part of France that had belonged to England. Mary was not a popular queen. She died of cancer in 1558 after ruling England for just five years.

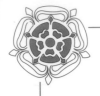

ELIZABETH 1

Elizabeth was very attractive when she was young. People called her Gloriana or the Faery (fairy) Queen to flatter her. When she got older, her hair went grey and she wore a red wig, which all the ladies of the court copied.

Mary did not have any children so her sister, Elizabeth, became queen. She was clever and ruled England well for 45 years. Like her father she had red hair and a temper, and she enjoyed music and dancing. But she was more like her grandfather, Henry VII, in the way she ruled. Her special adviser was William Cecil. Parliament was becoming more important and there was a struggle for power between members of Parliament and the Queen, who wanted to limit their rights to freedom of speech.

Elizabeth was a Protestant. She had seen how the people suffered under Edward's and Mary's religious laws. She tried to make the Church of England in to one where everybody could agree. Mary Queen of Scots, Elizabeth's cousin, was a Catholic. Elizabeth was afraid that the Catholics would try to make Mary the queen of England so she helped to make Scotland Protestant so that they would not support Mary. When the Protestants made Mary's son, James VI, king of Scotland in 1567, Mary fled to England. Elizabeth put Mary in prison to prevent her from plotting against her and, later, she had Mary beheaded.

Elizabeth did not have enough money. She could not afford to keep all Henry's palaces and the money for the court had to come out of her purse. Elizabeth could not afford wars and tried to avoid them but, when English ships began to compete with the Spanish, it ended in a war (see pages 12 and 13).

The English tried to put Ireland under English rule. They began to have colonies or 'plantations' there that were loyal to England but the Irish people fought against the English to keep their independence and their Catholic faith. Elizabeth helped the people of Holland who were fighting the Spanish. King Philip of Spain had his revenge by helping the Irish against England.

Elizabeth never married. Many foreign kings and ambitious Englishmen wanted to marry her but she said that she was married to England. When she died, the Scottish king, James, became king of England, Scotland and Wales.

Clothes

Elizabeth was not very rich but the queen had to look grand. She had 3000 dresses! They would have been made of silk or velvet, often decorated with gold embroidery or jewels.

We know what rich people wore because they had their portraits painted. Some of the richest clothes were kept because they were so valuable and can still be seen today. We do not know what poor people wore because there are so few pictures of them and their clothes wore out and were not kept. Sometimes shoes are found because they were hidden in houses to bring good luck.

Ordinary people wore wool or linen clothes, coloured with plant dyes. Women wore cotton caps indoors and, when they went out, put on a hat over their cap. Men and women wore ruffs or collars stiffened with wire or starch, which was introduced in 1564. Wealthy men usually wore linen shirts with a collar or ruff. Over this, they wore a doublet, a padded, fitted jacket, fastened with buttons. Sometimes they wore a cloak over this. Men's breeches went down to the knee or were shorter, padded 'trunk hose'. Men wore stockings which went up to their hose. Children wore the same style of clothes as their parents.

This shows what a Tudor merchant and his family might have worn.

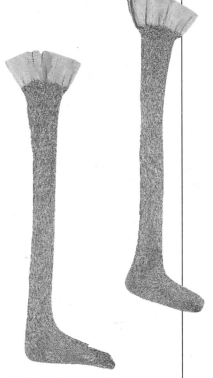

Hat, gloves and stockings which may have belonged to Elizabeth I. Luxury items like these came from Spain, France and Italy.

BATTLES AND ADVENTURES AT SEA

Henry VIII built bigger and stronger warships than any before. The *Sovereign* had guns on the deck which could fire 1188 metres (1300 yards). The guns took so long to re-load that they could only fire two shots an hour.

Building ships

Medieval ships were small. Tudor ships were built bigger to go further and had more sails, which could adapt to various winds. Merchants built their own ships to take their goods abroad for sale. They lost everything if their ships sank as there was no insurance. Henry VII helped towards the cost of shipbuilding and Elizabeth encouraged merchant shipping. Henry VII also built warships and he made the first dry dock in 1496, at Portsmouth. Henry VIII built more warships, such as *The Great Harry*, the largest in the world. By Elizabeth's reign, the Navy needed new ships. Sir John Hawkins had been a merchant, a slave-trader and a pirate. In 1578, he was made head of the Navy and he built new, fast ships that were easy to manage.

Life on board

Sailors had a terrible life on board. They had to sleep on the deck until, in 1597, the idea of using hammocks was copied from the native Americans. The food on ships was salted beef and fish, bread, dry biscuits and cheese. The food often had maggots in it and the drinking water went stale. On long journeys, many sailors died of scurvy because they did not have enough vitamin C from fresh fruit and vegetables. In 1601, the ships of the East India Company were the first to take lemons and oranges on voyages, to prevent scurvy.

War with Spain

In 1577-78 Francis Drake became the first Englishman to sail round the world. He went to South America to raid the Spanish ports and took so much gold that he changed the name of his ship to the *Golden Hind*. He explored up the West coast of America and then sailed west across the Pacific. He took an artist with him to make maps on the way. Of his crew of 164, only 47 survived. When Drake returned, Elizabeth went on board his ship and made him a knight.

In 1588 Philip II of Spain sent a fleet to invade England. It was called the Armada. English ships followed the Armada up the English Channel, firing at them. The Spanish ships stopped in Calais harbour and, during the night, the English set fire to six old ships and sent these 'fireships' among the Armada. The Spanish panicked and the English shot at them as they tried to escape. Fourteen of the Spanish ships were sunk or run aground and the rest fled to Ireland, where they were destroyed by a storm. The English Navy with its well-designed ships was now the most powerful and the English began to build their own empire all over the world.

*F*rancisco Drac is one of the greatest mariners that sails the seas.

A Spaniard taken prisoner by Francis Drake

This is a picture of the Armada. Can you see one ship sinking and a rowing boat rescuing the people?

The *Mary Rose*

The *Mary Rose* was one of Henry VIII's warships and had rows of low portholes from which guns could fire at enemy ships. In a sea battle when the French attacked Portsmouth, the *Mary Rose* turned too sharply and seawater flooded in through the portholes. The *Mary Rose* sank and most of the crew of 400 drowned. In the 1960s divers found the wreck of the ship and, in the 1980s, the wreck was brought to the surface. The divers found many of the sailors' possessions, preserved by the water. They included bows and arrows, guns, swords, knives, games, clothes, cooking pots and compasses. You can see these things, and the *Mary Rose*, at the Mary Rose Museum in Portsmouth.

The picture on the left shows tools found on the *Mary Rose*. They were used by carpenters who repaired the ship when it got damaged. On the right are some of the sailors' possessions, including a comb, a whistle and a rosary, as well as counters for playing games.

EXPLORERS AND TRADERS

The spice trade

Spices like pepper, cloves, nutmeg and cinnamon were used in cooking to give more flavour to the food. European merchants went to Constantinople to buy spices, which came from far away places like India and the Spice Islands in the Pacific Ocean. Spices were very expensive because they came from so far away. When Constantinople was taken over by the Turks in 1453, European merchants were afraid that they would no longer be able to buy spices. They tried to find a way of getting to the countries where the spices grew.

In 1498 a Portuguese explorer, Vasco da Gama, became the first European to sail to India. He wanted to buy pepper but the Muslim merchants stopped him from trading. In 1502 he went back with guns and the Portuguese trading empire in India and the East began.

At this time, people argued about how big the world was and the size and shape of the continents. Christopher Columbus believed that he could sail west instead of east and go round the world to reach the Spice Islands. He did not know that America was in the way. Columbus asked European monarchs to give him money for his expedition. Henry VII refused but Queen Isabella of Spain gave Columbus ships. In 1492 Columbus discovered some islands which he called West Indies because he thought he had reached India. He had found America, which he claimed for Spain, and the Spanish founded a great empire in South America.

Henry VII helped John Cabot, a sailor who was hoping to sail west to China. Cabot landed in Newfoundland, in Canada, in 1496 and claimed it for England. A Portuguese sailor called Ferdinand Magellan set sail in 1519 and became the first explorer to sail round the world. Magellan died on the journey and only 18 of his crew survived.

In 1554 three ships tried to get to China round Lapland. One sailor, Richard

It's true!

Raleigh was the first person to bring tobacco back to Britain. It was smoked in clay pipes with a very small bowl because it cost so much. An ounce cost as much as two or three days' wages.

European ships landing in Florida. The native Americans on the shore are armed with bows and arrows but the explorers had guns.

Chancellor, went on to Moscow where he met Czar Ivan the Terrible. The Muscovy company began to trade between Russia and England and Queen Elizabeth and the Czar wrote to each other in Latin.

The Portuguese and then the Dutch controlled the pepper trade with India. When the price of pepper trebled in 1601, the English founded the East India Company, which was the start of the British Empire in the East.

Colonies

The English set up colonies in Ireland and then started settlements in America. Sir Walter Raleigh went to Virginia in 1584 but the settlers could not grow enough food and had to rely on the native Americans to feed them. Soon after, the settlers gave up and disappeared without a trace.

Finding the way

During the 1500s people in different countries were working out new ideas in mathematics and measuring and map-making. Instruments for finding the way at sea helped mariners to find new lands. They measured the angle of the sun to know how far south and north they were but the distance east and west was more guess work. Maps and charts of the world were made. Mercator, a Dutch map maker, made a map of the world in 1569. We still use his way of showing the round world as a flat map.

An astrolabe helped sailors to navigate by finding the position of the Sun, Moon and stars.

This map shows what people knew of the world. They did not know the exact shape and size of some lands.

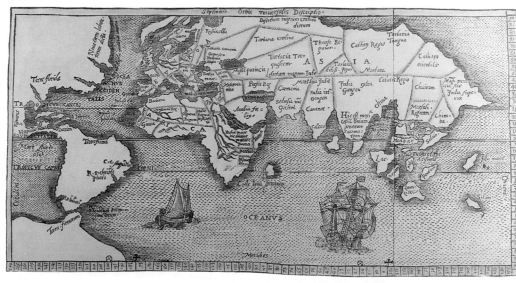

A compass helped sailors to know which direction they were facing but it was not very accurate.

EVERYDAY LIFE

The riches of England are greater than those of any other country in Europe.

In Wales They take great delight in large herds of cattle, and most of them live upon the produce of their dairies. Their towns are few and small; most people live separately in the country.

Scotland is marvellously mountainous, sterile, rugged and marshy.

In Ireland The soil is good and would be productive if better cultivated. Merchants sell leather, linen, woollen cloth, metals and good horses. The natives are warlike.

Calendar of Venetian State Papers

England looked very different from today. Most of the country was farmland or woodland and the tall oak trees which grew in the woods were used to build ships and houses. The king owned huge areas of forest called royal parks where he hunted deer and wild boar. Ordinary people were not allowed to go in them.

Only one in 20 people lived in a town and the towns were tiny. Most lived in villages or farms in the north and west. Sometimes, so many people died from the plague that a village would become empty and disappear.

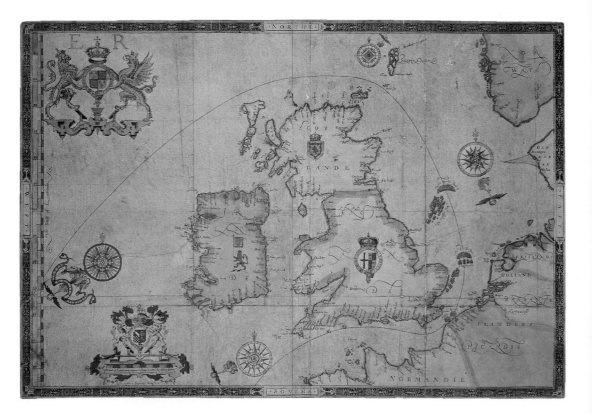

On this Tudor map, England and Wales are one country and Scotland and Ireland are separate. Tudor maps do not show roads.

Farming

Ninety per cent of the population lived by farming. The fields were divided up so that everybody got a share of the good land. There were no hedges round the fields. There were common fields where all the villagers had the right to let their animals eat the grass. Many people kept a cow and made butter and cheese to sell in the market. Others kept flocks of geese which could be eaten; their feathers could be made into quills for people to write with and goose grease could be used to make things waterproof. Pigs were allowed to wander in the woods. They were much more like wild boars than the pigs seen in farms today.

Planting crops was hard work. Farmers ploughed their field strips with oxen and then pulled a harrow over the ground to break up the lumps. When the corn was ripe, it had to be cut with sickles and made into sheaves (bundles) with string. Then it had to be taken into the barn to be kept dry. The lord of the area would take some as a tax and so would the priest. The rest was ground up into flour at the mill, and the miller would take some in payment.

The men who worked on the land were called husbandmen. They had very little money and had to live on what they grew. Only one in ten people could read. Yeoman farmers, who owned the farms, were beginning to grow richer. They were better educated and four in ten of them could read. The development of printing (see page 23) meant that there were books which contained new ideas on farming.

A man measuring corn. There were strict rules about how corn should be measured to stop people being cheated.

Sheep

More and more landowners were farming sheep instead of growing wheat because they could sell the wool abroad for a good price. The landowners needed more land, so they fenced in the land where their tenants had kept their animals and grown crops. Whole villages sometimes disappeared and were replaced by fields of sheep. The tenants moved to other areas, looking for work in the towns, and some became homeless beggars.

A farmer planting leeks. People from Holland showed the English how to grow better vegetables.

Sheep have ate up our meadows and our downs,
Our corn, our wood, whole villages and towns.

The Poems of Reverend Thomas Bastard

It's true!

Sir Walter Raleigh introduced potatoes to Ireland. They eventually became Ireland's most important crop.

HOMES RICH AND POOR

Until the 15th century, wealthy people lived in castles. By the late 1500s times were more peaceful and rich people began to build houses for comfort and style rather than safety. As England became more wealthy in the 1500s, houses improved. Most were made of wood but some were brick, with glass windows and chimneys.

Henry VIII's minister, Wolsey, had Hampton Court Palace built for himself but he gave it to Henry to keep in his good books!

A Tudor merchant or yeoman's house would be made of big oak beams. The walls were often made of 'wattle and daub'. Wattle was wooden panels (like a fence) and daub was plaster. All but the largest houses were made of wood. It was easy for wooden houses to catch fire. In a town, fire could spread very quickly. There were no fire engines and people had to put out a fire with buckets of water.

> *By misadventure of fire (which) happened within the town of Nantwich in the County of Chester upon the tenth day of December last, there was burnt ... to the number of 800 houses (more likely about 150), with the most part of the household stuff of the inhabitants ... and the town became desolate.*
>
> A letter from Queen Elizabeth I (1584)

This farmhouse is made from wood, with a hall in the middle. It has no chimney and smoke from the fire escaped through the roof.

It's true!

In 1589 Sir John Harington had the first water closet (lavatory) installed in his house near Bath – the idea took 200 years to catch on!

Because glass was expensive, it became a symbol of wealth. Windows were made by blowing bubbles of glass and cutting them up into diamond shapes. These were then fixed together with lead strips. Poorer people had windows without glass, which were covered with shutters at night or when it was cold.

Poor families often lived in just one room with a ladder leading to a loft. The poorest people could not afford barns and had to share their home with their animals. People who could not afford to own a house had to rent one.

In larger houses, the walls were covered with wood panelling, tapestries or painted cloth. Wealthy people had furniture like chairs, tables and cupboards or chests. They began to sleep in beds with a wooden frame, sometimes with curtains and a mattress of flock (wool) or feathers. Poor families slept on straw mattresses on the floor. Ordinary people did not have chairs but sat on benches. Sometimes, children had to stand during meals because they didn't have enough chairs or benches.

In most homes water was brought in from a well and washing was done in the river. By the end of the 16th century some very rich people had water piped to their houses.

In the early 16th century, many houses had no chimneys and the fire was laid on stones in the middle of the floor. Smoke made the roof black with soot. By the end of the century houses began to have chimneys. The more chimneys a house had, the richer the owner was.

> There are old men dwelling in the village ... which have noted the multitude of chimneys lately erected, whereas in their young days there were not above two or three in most towns.
>
> William Harrison *Description of England* (1577)

Rich people planted gardens next to their houses. The fashion was to have small beds of flowers or herbs enclosed by tiny hedges. The flower beds made patterns and the gardens were called knot gardens. They were surrounded by gravel paths where people liked to walk.

This yeoman's house is made of flint and has a thatched roof and a chimney. The windows are very small because glass was expensive.

The Tudors grew many herbs and used them in cooking, as medicines and to make perfumes.

LIFE IN THE TOWN

Most Tudor towns were very small, with only a few hundred houses, but they were growing. London was the largest town in Britain. At the beginning of the Tudor period, there were about 70,000 people living there. By the time Elizabeth I died, the population of London had trebled.

Foreign trade

Very few English people went abroad and they were suspicious of foreigners. In Henry VIII's reign there was a riot in London against foreigners. Henry had the rioters hanged to show foreign merchants that it was safe to come to England.

> *London is a large, excellent and mighty city of business and the most important in the whole kingdom: most of the inhabitants are employed in buying and selling merchandise and trading in almost every corner of the world. ...The inhabitants are magnificently dressed and are extremely proud; and because the trades-people seldom go into other countries, but always remain in their houses in the city attending to their business, they care little for foreigners, but scoff and laugh at them.*
>
> Jacob Rathgeb, a German who visited London in 1592

This map shows that London was still surrounded by fields. You can see how busy the Thames river was.

The streets of the towns were crowded and filthy. There were no proper drains or sewers and people threw rubbish into the street. The dirt attracted rats and mice which spread disease. There were epidemics and many people, especially children, died. The streets in a town smelled terrible and rich people often carried a little bag of herbs called a pomander.

Crime

Local government began under the Tudors. Each town elected a mayor and a council. Constables and bailiffs were also elected to enforce the law. For example, they tested the weights used by bakers and shopkeepers to make sure that they were not cheating people.

There was no police force so few criminals were caught but, when they were, they were severely punished. They could be whipped, burned to death, branded with hot metal, beheaded or hanged.

The poor

In the 1500s more and more people were becoming unemployed and homeless. They included orphans, the elderly, wounded soldiers and tenants whose land had been taken away. The monasteries had helped to look after poor people but, after the dissolution of the monasteries (see page 8), the poor could only live by begging.

> *They live in the streets in the dirt ... and die like dogs or beasts without any mercy showed them at all.*
>
> Philip Stubbes *The Anatomie of Abuses* (1593)

Anybody who was caught doing wrong was likely to be put in the stocks. Their feet were locked into holes in the wood. People often threw things at criminals in the stocks.

Rich people began to build houses for the old who were poor. Many of these almshouses can still be seen today.

People were afraid that the towns would become full of beggars and crime would increase. Parliament passed laws to have beggars whipped and sent back to the place they had come from. Britain was the first country to set up a system of help for the poor. A 'poor tax' was collected in the towns but it was only for people who could not work, like the blind or the ill. The old were expected to go on working until they became too old or ill. Some people gave money to charity to build almshouses for the old or 'hospitals' for orphans.

📖 Words, words, words ....

Hark, hark, the dogs do bark,
The beggars are coming to town ...
is a nursery rhyme describing the crowds of beggars in the big towns like Norwich, Bristol, and London.

It's true!
Henry VIII had 72,000 vagabonds (homeless beggars) hanged.

Britain sold a great deal of wool to other countries. Raw wool was sold to France, where it was made into cloth. Some wool was made into cloth in Britain. There were strict rules to keep the quality high.

People in the country went to market with the things they had to sell. On market days stalls were set up. Some of the stalls were made more permanent and became shops. Usually there was a row of butchers, a row of fishmongers, and so on. Streets were often named after the type of shop found there, such as Pudding Lane or Threadneedle Street.

These merchants are buying and selling wool and food. One merchant is checking the quality of the goods he is about to buy.

Towns were centres for trade. Food, clothes, crafts and luxury items were all brought into towns on foot, by horse and cart or up rivers like the Thames. Merchants from all over the country and from abroad came to the largest towns to trade.

Craftsmen joined together to form guilds, which kept up the standards of their trade. People needed new skills and Henry VIII asked craftsmen from Italy to come and show the British how to make iron cannon and glass. The English learnt to make all sorts of things, like pins, needles and buttons, instead of importing them.

Wages were kept low by law, even when prices were high. People worked from about 6 am to 7 pm but there were long breaks for breakfast, lunch and 'noon-day'. The pace of work was slow and workers were even allowed a half an hour snooze after lunch!

Words, words, words ....

When cloth was made up, it was washed and stretched out to dry, pulled tight on 'tenterhooks'. We say that somebody who is anxiously waiting is 'on tenterhooks'.

The building on the left is a shop. The building on the right is a hall where people set up market stalls.

Travel

Most people did not travel very far in their lifetime. The average person probably did not go much further then the next big town and only traders and explorers went abroad. Ordinary people walked, rode on a horse or travelled in a horse-drawn cart. The roads were badly made and had deep holes. It took a fortnight to go by road from Edinburgh to London. Some wagons began to make a regular service between towns. The first coaches were made in England in the 1550s but they did not catch on as they were very bumpy. When springs were invented in the 1630s, coaches became more comfortable.

Many people travelled by boat because the roads were so bad and goods were also carried around the country in this way. Londoners used barges like taxis, as the Thames was a better highway than the narrow crowded streets of London. It cost one penny to be ferried across the river.

Here, people are paying a toll to enter the town, where they will sell their goods. The sheep, pigs and cattle have been brought to town to sell for meat.

Printing

William Caxton was the first person to print books in Britain. Printed books 'made in one daye' (as Caxton printed on his first book) were cheaper than books which had to be copied out by hand. The new books were printed on paper which had been made by hand from old linen rags. The first paper mill producing large amounts of paper for printing was opened in Hertford in 1495. Paper mills produced paper more quickly by beating up the rags to make fibres. Paper was costly and did not become cheaper until the 1850s. There were no newspapers in England until 1621. One of the first newspapers was made in 1566 in Venice, Italy.

Printing meant that new ideas spread much more quickly and books spread knowledge in subjects of all kinds. In 1525 the first textbooks appeared. They were about metals and mining, farming and geometry. Understanding ideas about mathematics and measuring was important for builders, surveyors and map-makers. In 1536 the first printed Bible, translated into English by Miles Coverdale, was printed in London.

It's true!

When Britain was a Catholic country there were plenty of holydays (holidays) – as many as 50 a year!

WHAT PEOPLE ATE

Today, supermarkets sell food from all over the world. In Tudor times, people ate whatever they could grow so their meals were made up of bread, milk, butter, cheese and, sometimes, some meat or fish. Cooking was usually done over an open wood fire in a cauldron, a large cooking pot. Meat was cooked over a fire on a spit, like a barbecue.

In the summer there was plenty of food. People could eat fruit, vegetables and other crops. But they had to store some of the food for winter, when there would be less to eat. Drying was the only way of preserving fruit and vegetables. Meat was smoked in the chimney and fish could be salted. The Norwegians freeze-dried cod during their cold winters and sold it to the English. People who could afford them used spices to add flavour to their food.

These people are enjoying a feast. A visitor to England said how dirty the houses were. Can you see all the bones on the floor?

These dishes were found on the *Mary Rose.* They are made of a metal called pewter and were easier to clean than wooden plates.

Tea and coffee didn't come to England until the next century, so people drank beer, even for breakfast. Chidren had milk or 'milk sops' (bread and milk).

*T**he general drink is beer, which is prepared from barley, and is exceedingly well tasted.***
Paul Hentzner *A Journey into England* (1598)

Words, words, words ....

The Tudor court liked practical jokes. They would cook an empty pie and then put live birds or frogs in it so that they jumped out when the pie was served. This is what the nursery rhyme Sing a Song of Sixpence is about:

Sing a song of sixpence, a pocket full of rye
Four and twenty blackbirds baked in a pie.
When the pie was opened the birds began to sing.
Wasn't that a dainty dish to set before a king?

Many of the foods that we eat today were not known to the Tudors. When explorers began to travel to America, they brought back new types of food. The first turkeys were eaten in England in 1525 and the first potatoes in 1586.

Sugar was very dear so it was a status symbol. At the end of a meal, Tudor lords and ladies would eat a sweet course called the 'banquet' in a 'banqueting house' in the garden. They ate Turkish delight, jellies and sweet cakes. Queen Elizabeth is said to have had bad teeth because she ate too much sugar. The Spanish started to plant sugar in the West Indies in 1506 and sugar from America became cheaper. The owners of plantations began to use slaves from Africa, which is how the slave trade began.

A rich household would have servants to prepare the food. Oranges and lemons came from the Mediterranean and only the rich could afford them.

THE COURT

Henry VIII sitting on his throne, surrounded by his councillors

Tudor kings and queens spent most of their time at their London palaces at Whitehall and Greenwich. The work of running the country was done by the monarch with the advice of their Council. The Council also acted as the highest court of justice to which anyone could appeal if they thought they had been unfairly treated. The monarch could call Parliament together to make laws or approve taxes.

Hundreds of people lived or worked at the palace: the Council, government officials, servants and guards. They were known as the Court. Ambassadors from other countries visited the Court. All the money from taxes and fines went to the king or queen who paid for all the palaces, the wages of the staff and the food.

In the summer, the Court made a 'progress' around parts of England. They stayed at the houses of wealthy subjects which cost the subjects a lot of money because the Court could be as many as 1000 people! In 1577 Queen Elizabeth and her court went to Gorhambury, St. Albans to stay with Sir Nicholas Bacon. They stayed for four days and ate: 8 oxen, 60 sheep, 18 calves, 34 lambs, 206 capons (fattened chickens), 380 chickens, 120 geese, 152 herons, 103 bitterns and godwits, as well as pheasants, partridges, quails, mallards, teals, curlews, sea fish, bacon, cows' udders and calves' feet. It cost £577 six shillings and seven pence farthing (£577.33).

The Court enjoyed entertainments such as feasts, plays, music and dancing. Everybody enjoyed music. Henry VIII composed music and Elizabeth I played the lute (a musical instrument like a guitar) and the virginals (a keyboard like a piano). The English were famous for their songs called madrigals. The music of Tudor composers such as Thomas Tallis, William Byrd and John Dowland is still enjoyed today.

It's true!

The first firework display in Britain was arranged to entertain Queen Elizabeth at Temple Fields, Warwickshire in August, 1572.

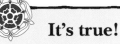

HEALTH

Life was short for Tudor people. Doctors could not cure many of the diseases they can treat today. Many people died of illnesses like measles, smallpox and influenza. It was often children who died. King Edward died of tuberculosis when he was just 15. If the weather was bad and the crops failed people died of starvation.

Doctors were beginning to learn from books and to find out more about the human body from treating wounded soldiers. Some people thought that dissecting (cutting up) bodies was wrong but the Royal College of Surgeons was allowed to do this after 1565.

Barbers pulled out bad teeth and did operations, as well as shaving people and cutting their hair. If a barber treated somebody with the plague, other customers could be infected so, eventually, the Guild of Barber Surgeons became doctors and ordinary barbers just cut hair.

These two syringes were found on the *Mary Rose*. They were in the medical chest of the barber surgeon with 62 other items.

It's true!

Handkerchiefs were first used at this time, and were mostly wafted about for show. People thought that blowing your nose in a handkerchief was rather disgusting.

If a man be sick of a fever, it is some comfort that he can take a bed-staff (stick) and knock, and his servant comes up and helps him with a cordial (a soothing drink). But if a man be sick of the plague, then he sits and lies all alone.

William Bridge (a preacher)

📖 Words, words, words ....

Ring-o'-ring-o'-roses
A pocket full of posies
Atishoo atishoo
We all fall down

This nursery rhyme is all about the plague. The 'ring o' roses' was a rash of sores. People thought that the plague came from bad air, so they carried posies of sweet-smelling flowers to protect themselves. Sneezing was a sign that someone had the plague. The plague could kill a person in a day – 'We all fall down'. People who had the plague were avoided because others were afraid of catching it. In 1603 30,000 people died of plague in London.

Doctors dissecting a body. They learned how the body works by looking at corpses.

It's true!

The first toothbrush was made in 1496.

HOW CHILDREN LIVED

Children had to grow up fast in Tudor times but they did have some time for play. There are pictures of children playing marbles and wealthy children had toys. Most poor children had to work hard helping their parents at home. Boys helped with growing food and tending the animals and girls learned how to cook, spin and weave.

Lord Cobham's children playing. They have a monkey, a parrot, a chaffinch, a little dog and a toy with bells.

Education

Few people could read or write and many signed their name with X. Although printing made books cheaper, most people still could not afford them. Some children were taught to read and write by the village priest and rich parents employed a tutor to teach their children at home. Queen Elizabeth and her brother King Edward grew up together and shared the same lessons. Elizabeth was very clever and could speak Latin, Greek, Italian, French and Spanish.

Schoolmasters whipped children who were badly behaved. King Edward's teachers were not allowed to beat him because he was going to be king. When Edward was naughty, the teacher beat a 'whipping boy', Barnaby Fitzpatrick, instead!

Before Henry VIII destroyed the monasteries, many of them had run schools for boys. These were replaced by schools set up by wealthy families. They were called 'grammar' schools because Latin grammar was the main subject. They charged fees but some poor boys were taught there as well. Lessons started at 6 am in summer and 7 am in winter, and went on until 4 pm or 5 pm in the afternoon.

The teacher has a cane to make sure the boys behave!

Children were often sent to other people's houses to learn. Boys also went as apprentices to learn a craft or trade such as carpentry. Girls often became servants.

> Y ou can see how little affection the English have for their children; for after having them at home till the age of seven or nine years they put them out, both males and females, to hard service in the houses of other people, generally for another seven or nine years. These are called apprentices.

Calendar of Venetian State Papers (c. 1498)

Entertainment

Life was rough and cruel and so were many of the popular sports. People enjoyed cock fighting, dog fights and bull fights. Sometimes dogs were set to fight a bear. People placed bets on which would win. Wealthy people practised for war by jousting, tilting and fencing and they had many competitions to see who was the best. People also enjoyed going to watch criminals being put to death.

Other games and sports included bowls, board games like backgammon and gambling games with playing cards or dice.

The Tudors enjoyed fairs and fetes, with acrobats, jugglers and people doing tricks. Many fairs travelled around the country entertaining people. Groups of actors also travelled round the country. They stayed at inns and performed plays in the courtyards. An actor, James Burbage, built the first theatre in London in 1577. In the 1590s The Globe, the Swan and the Rose theatres were built in Southwark in London. Recently, the Rose Theatre has been excavated by a team of archaeologists. Some of Shakespeare's plays were first acted there.

Backgammon was a popular game in Tudor times and is still played today.

This picture shows a fete and you can see the different clothes people might have worn. There are musicians and dancers. Can you see the spits of roasting meat in the kitchen?

29

Index

Glossary

allies   supporters
annull   cancel out
brand   to mark with piece of hot metal
cauldron   a large metal cooking pot
cordial   a warming drink
cut purse   a thief
daub   a type of plaster
dissect   to take to pieces
dissolution   destruction
doublet   a man's tight jacket
excavate   to dig up
excommunicate   to expel from the church
farthingale   a hooped petticoat

flock   wool or cotton stuffing
guild   group of merchants and craftsmen
lute   a musical instrument like a guitar
monarch   a king or queen
pomander   a ball of sweet-smelling substances
Reformation   a period of change in the Church
scurvy   a disease caused by lack of vitamin C
sheaves   bundles
toll   a tax for using a road or river
traitor   a person who betrays his country
treaty   an agreement
vagabond   a homeless beggar
wattle   wooden panels used to build houses